# CORAL REEFS

SQUIRRELFISH   6-12 in.

MOON JELLY
6 - 16 in.

QUEEN TRIGGER FISH
8-16 in.

BLUE CHROMIS
3-4 in.

GLASSY SWEEPER 3-5in

BANDED BUTTERFLYFISH  3-5in.

CARIBBEAN
REEF SQUID
6-12 in.

BALLOONFISH  8-14 in.

SERGEANT MAJOR
4-6 in.

SPOTTED CLEANER SHRIMP
.75-1 in.

INDIGO HAMLET
3-4.5 in.

COMMON OCTOPUS
15 - 28 in.

RED CORAL CRAB  3.5-4.5 in.

COMMON SEA FAN
2-6 ft.

BUSHY SEA WHIP  1-2 ft.

STAGHORN CORAL
1-8 ft.

ELKHORN CORAL   3-12 f

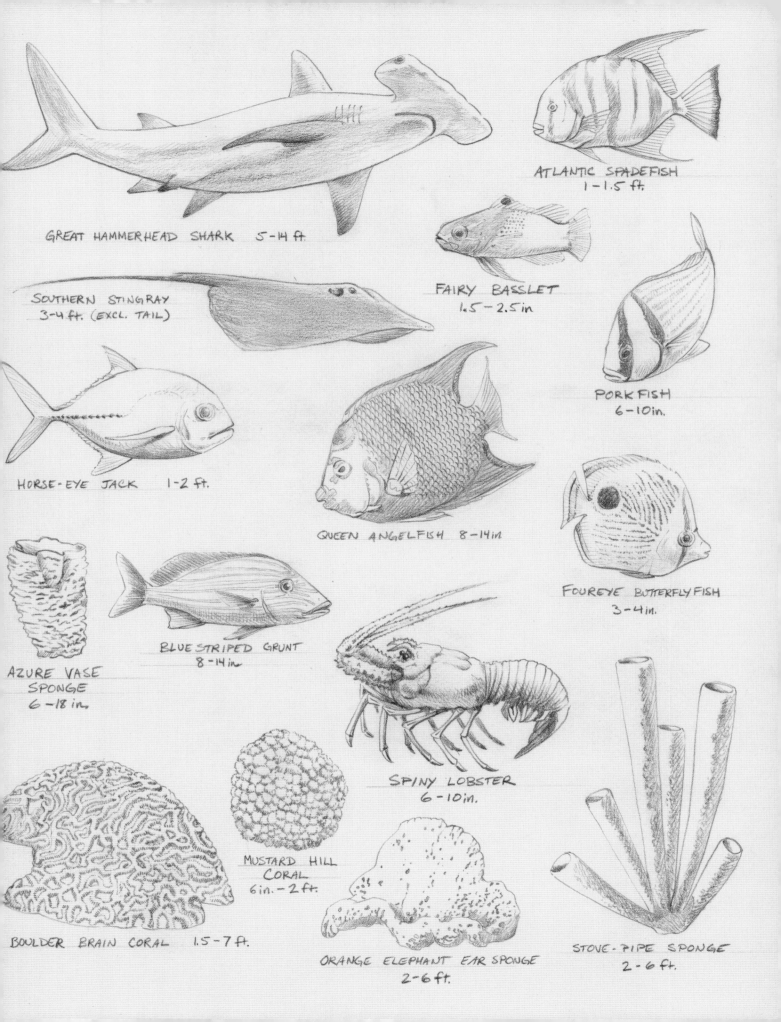

GREAT HAMMERHEAD SHARK   5-14 ft.

ATLANTIC SPADEFISH
1-1.5 ft.

FAIRY BASSLET
1.5-2.5 in

SOUTHERN STINGRAY
3-4 ft. (EXCL. TAIL)

PORKFISH
6-10in.

HORSE-EYE JACK   1-2 ft.

QUEEN ANGELFISH 8-14in

FOUREYE BUTTERFLY FISH
3-4in.

AZURE VASE
SPONGE
6-18 in.

BLUE STRIPED GRUNT
8-14 in.

SPINY LOBSTER
6-10in.

MUSTARD HILL
CORAL
6in.-2 ft.

BOULDER BRAIN CORAL   1.5-7 ft.

ORANGE ELEPHANT EAR SPONGE
2-6 ft.

STOVE-PIPE SPONGE
2-6 ft.

For Liam

Special thanks to Ann M. Tarrant, assistant scientist, Woods Hole Oceanographic Institution; Linda K. Dybas, Watson Bartlett professor of biology, Knox College; and Stela Sore

An imprint of Macmillan Publishing Group, LLC
175 Fifth Avenue • New York, NY 10010
mackids.com

Square Fish and the Square Fish logo are trademarks of Macmillan and are used by Roaring Brook Press under license from Macmillan.

Our books may be purchased in bulk for promotional, educational, or business use. Please contact your local bookseller or the Macmillan Corporate and Premium Sales Department at (800) 221-7945 ext. 5442 or by e-mail at MacmillanSpecialMarkets@macmillan.com.

Library of Congress Cataloging-in-Publication Data

Chin, Jason, 1978-
    Coral reefs / Jason Chin.
        p. cm.
    "A Neal Porter Book."
    ISBN 978-1-250-07948-0 (paperback)
    1. Coral reefs and islands—Juvenile literature. 2. Coral reef
ecology—Juvenile literature. I. Title.
    GB461.C45 2011
    577.7'89—dc22
                            2010045189

Originally published in the United States by Roaring Brook Press
First Square Fish Edition: 2016
Square Fish logo designed by Filomena Tuosto

10 9 8 7 6

AR: 0.5 / LEXILE: 1010L

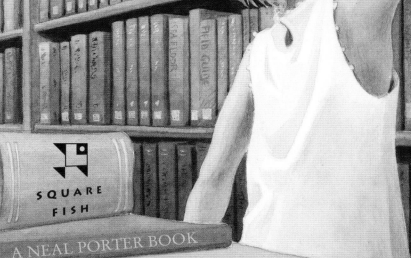

JASON CHIN

# CORAL REEFS

CORAL REE

SQUARE
FISH

A NEAL PORTER BOOK

ROARING BROOK PRESS/*New York*

For more than 400 million years, corals have been building reefs in the earth's oceans. Corals may look like plants, but they are actually animals. Some are soft and sway back and forth in the water, while others, called hard corals, are rigid. Corals are made up of polyps, and most have hundreds of tiny polyps on their surface.

Each polyp has stinging tentacles that it can extend to catch food. The polyps of hard corals build a limestone skeleton and live in indentations, or cups, along its surface. When a polyp is in danger, it can retract into its cup for protection. Hard corals are able to build their skeletons because of a remarkable partnership that they have with a type of algae. The algae live inside the polyp and, working together, the polyp and the algae build the coral's skeleton.

There are thousands of kinds of coral, and each species has a different shape and color. Some have intricate branches, while others grow in mounds on the ocean floor. When a coral's polyps die, they decay, but the skeleton remains and new corals can grow on top of it.

Over hundreds of years, the coral piles up and spreads across the seafloor, eventually forming a living mountain called a coral reef. Corals may be small, but they are incredible builders. Coral reefs are the largest structures built by any animal on earth— the Belize barrier reef is over 180 miles long!

Coral reefs are home to thousands of plants and animals. There are so many species living in reefs that they are often called the cities of the sea.

These aquatic cities grow in tropical waters around the world. They start close to shore and extend out into the ocean.

Different parts of the reef have different kinds of
animals. All of these animals interact in a complex
web of relationships, and each has its own
place in the system.

Many of the relationships are between predator and prey. Corals eat plankton, tiny organisms that float through the water. The polyps use their tentacles to catch the plankton so they can eat it.

But corals aren't just predators, they are also prey. Coral polyps retreat into their cups for protection, but that can't stop parrot fish. Parrot fish eat the algae that live inside the coral polyps. They use their special beaks to break through coral skeletons and gobble up the polyps inside.

The chain doesn't stop there—parrot fish are preyed on by larger fish, like groupers and sharks.

A series of species that eat each other (like the coral, parrot fish, and sharks) is called a food chain. There are many different food chains on the reef and all together they make up the food web.

Many species use the reef for protection. As the coral
grows, it creates many cracks and crevices in the
reef that make perfect hiding places for small fish.
Squirrelfish use the reef for protection when
predators like the Nassau grouper
are on the prowl.

In addition
to evading predators,
each species must also find food
to survive. Moray eels have slender
bodies that are perfectly adapted for
navigating the narrow nooks and crannies of
the reef. Hiding fish may be safe from groupers,
but they still have to watch out for hungry morays.

The sandy area between the reef and the shore is called the lagoon, and it is covered by beds of sea grass. The lagoon plays an important role in keeping the reef healthy. Puffer fish and sea horses are common in the lagoon. Many young fish take shelter in the sea grass before growing up and moving on to the reef. Rays visit the lagoon to hunt for shrimp and snails, and sea turtles eat the sea grass itself.

Beyond the lagoon, corals start to appear, marking the beginning of the reef. Groups of fish, called schools, can be found swimming over the reef. Fish swim in schools for protection and sometimes different species, such as white grunts and porkfish, will swim together to make an even bigger group. By working together, schooling fish have a better chance at survival.

Many species have developed unusual adaptations that help them survive. The scorpion fish barely resembles a fish as it sits on the seafloor waiting to ambush its prey. Predators had better watch out, too—on its back are spines filled with a painful venom, an effective defense.

The frogfish goes fishing for its dinner. It changes color to blend in with its surroundings and dangles a special fin in front of its mouth to lure its prey close. When an unsuspecting fish takes the bait, the frogfish attacks—and it rarely misses. The frogfish is one of the quickest fish in the ocean.

The common octopus has a few uncommon adaptations. It can change the color and the texture of its skin to blend in with any environment. Being a master of disguise is perfect for hunting and hiding.

If a predator does happen to find it, the octopus has a backup plan. It releases a cloud of ink that confuses its enemy. The scorpion fish, the frogfish, and the octopus are just a few of the many reef species with unique adaptations that aid in their survival.

Sometimes different species work together to help each other survive. Many large predators, like tiger groupers, have a partnership with tiny fish called neon gobies: the groupers visit the gobies for a cleaning. The gobies swim all over their customers, picking parasites and dead skin off their scales, gills, and fins. The groupers even let

the gobies swim inside their mouths to clean their teeth. This arrangement works out well for everyone. The gobies get a free meal, and the groupers get a cleaning.

At the end of the reef, the coral drops off dramatically into the depths. This is the reef wall, and beyond it is the open ocean. The tropical waters bordering reefs have very little life in them, making food scarce. Coral reefs, on the other hand,

are like oases in the desert. They are teeming
with life and provide feeding grounds for visitors.
The largest fish in the world, the whale shark,
visits the Belize barrier reef every spring
to feed on the microscopic eggs of
spawning reef fish.

More than four thousand kinds of fish and thousands of other species have been discovered in coral reefs—more than in any other part of the ocean. But that's not all. Scientists believe that reefs are home to millions of species that haven't been discovered yet! Remarkably, this enormous quantity of life is squeezed into just a fraction of the ocean. Coral reefs may be big, but they cover less than half a percent of the total ocean floor. With so many species living in such a small space, it's no wonder coral reefs are called cities of the sea.

Like all cities, reefs are busy places and they are full of thousands of different relationships. Many of these relationships are between predator and prey . . .

. . . while others are partnerships that benefit everyone.

All of these relationships make coral reefs some of the most complex ecosystems in the world. Each species has its place in the system, and all of them depend on the reef builders for their home:

the corals.

# The Threat to Coral Reefs

Corals have bright, beautiful colors, but their colors aren't all their own. Most corals are actually pale, and the colors we see come from the algae that live inside them. When corals are under stress they expel their algae and lose their color. Without the algae, most corals will eventually die. This is called coral bleaching, and it's becoming more and more common in the world's reefs. Corals are fragile creatures and they face many threats that cause them to bleach and otherwise imperil their survival. Some threats are natural, such as hurricanes. Others are human-made, such as pollution and over-fishing. The biggest threat to reefs today is rising levels of greenhouse gases, caused in part by the burning of fossil fuels. These gases are causing the world's oceans to warm up and become more acidic. Water that is too warm causes coral bleaching, and water that is too acidic makes it very difficult for corals to build their skeletons. These threats are global, so the damage isn't isolated to a few corals here and there—every coral in the world, and all the animals that depend on them, are in danger.

The prospects for reefs are gloomy, but there is a bright side: you can be part of the solution. Here are some things that you can do to help:

**Reduce, reuse, and recycle:** Every time something is made, energy is used. Most of that energy comes from fuels that generate greenhouse gases. If we can reduce the number of things we make, fewer greenhouse gases will be produced. You can participate by reducing the amount of things you buy, reusing the things you already have, and recycling the things you don't need anymore.

**Conserve water:** Water from our homes goes down the drain and often washes out into the ocean, bringing pollutants with it. Using less water means fewer pollutants will end up in the ocean.

**Leave the fish where they are:** If you buy a new fish for your fish tank, be sure it wasn't taken from a coral reef. If you visit a reef, don't take any fish or coral home with you.

**Walk, bike, or take the bus:** Greenhouse gases produced by automobiles endanger reefs. Consider walking, biking, or taking public transport instead of traveling by car.

**Educate yourself:** This book is just a start. The more you understand about coral reefs, the better you will be able to help them.

## CORAL REEF CROSS-SECTION

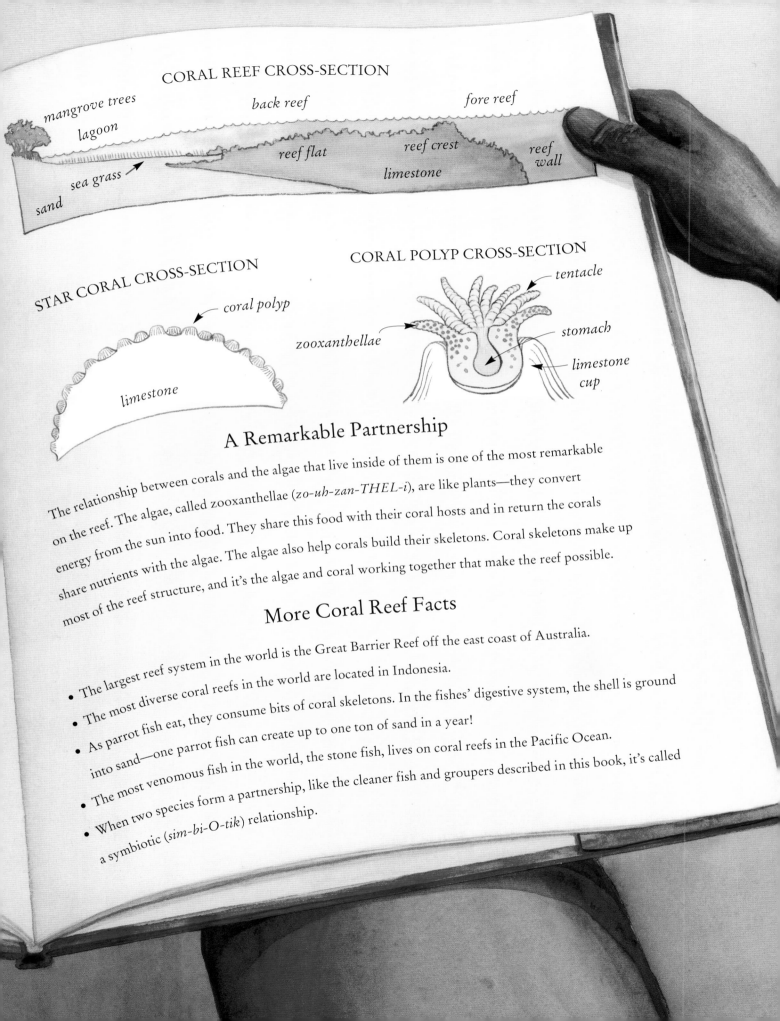

mangrove trees

back reef

fore reef

lagoon

reef flat

reef crest

reef wall

sea grass

limestone

sand

## STAR CORAL CROSS-SECTION

coral polyp

limestone

## CORAL POLYP CROSS-SECTION

tentacle

zooxanthellae

stomach

limestone cup

## A Remarkable Partnership

The relationship between corals and the algae that live inside of them is one of the most remarkable on the reef. The algae, called zooxanthellae (*zo-uh-zan-THEL-i*), are like plants—they convert energy from the sun into food. They share this food with their coral hosts and in return the corals share nutrients with the algae. The algae also help corals build their skeletons. Coral skeletons make up most of the reef structure, and it's the algae and coral working together that make the reef possible.

## More Coral Reef Facts

- The largest reef system in the world is the Great Barrier Reef off the east coast of Australia.
- The most diverse coral reefs in the world are located in Indonesia.
- As parrot fish eat, they consume bits of coral skeletons. In the fishes' digestive system, the shell is ground into sand—one parrot fish can create up to one ton of sand in a year!
- The most venomous fish in the world, the stone fish, lives on coral reefs in the Pacific Ocean.
- When two species form a partnership, like the cleaner fish and groupers described in this book, it's called a symbiotic (*sim-bi-O-tik*) relationship.

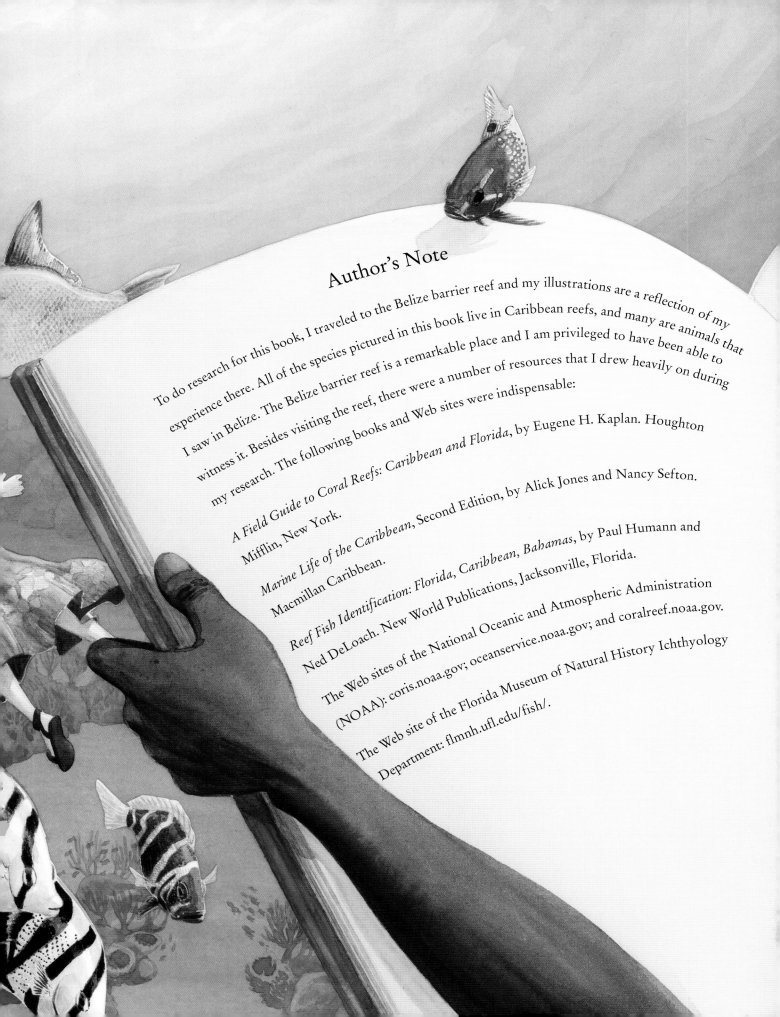

# Author's Note

To do research for this book, I traveled to the Belize barrier reef and my illustrations are a reflection of my experience there. All of the species pictured in this book live in Caribbean reefs, and many are animals that I saw in Belize. The Belize barrier reef is a remarkable place and I am privileged to have been able to witness it. Besides visiting the reef, there were a number of resources that I drew heavily on during my research. The following books and Web sites were indispensable:

*A Field Guide to Coral Reefs: Caribbean and Florida*, by Eugene H. Kaplan. Houghton Mifflin, New York.

*Marine Life of the Caribbean*, Second Edition, by Alick Jones and Nancy Sefton. Macmillan Caribbean.

*Reef Fish Identification: Florida, Caribbean, Bahamas*, by Paul Humann and Ned DeLoach. New World Publications, Jacksonville, Florida.

The Web sites of the National Oceanic and Atmospheric Administration (NOAA): coris.noaa.gov; oceanservice.noaa.gov; and coralreef.noaa.gov.

The Web site of the Florida Museum of Natural History Ichthyology Department: flmnh.ufl.edu/fish/ .

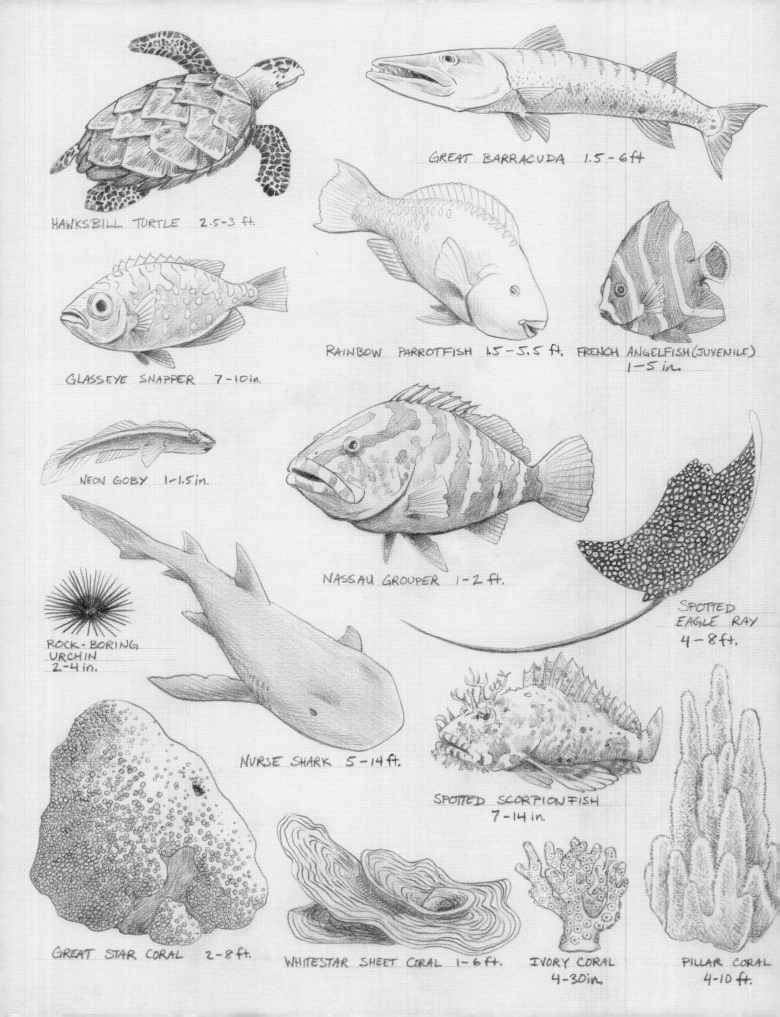

HAWKSBILL TURTLE   2.5-3 ft.

GREAT BARRACUDA   1.5-6 ft

GLASSEYE SNAPPER   7-10 in.

RAINBOW PARROTFISH   1.5-5.5 ft.   FRENCH ANGELFISH (JUVENILE) 1-5 in.

NEON GOBY   1-1.5 in.

NASSAU GROUPER   1-2 ft.

ROCK-BORING URCHIN 2-4 in.

NURSE SHARK   5-14 ft.

SPOTTED EAGLE RAY 4-8 ft.

SPOTTED SCORPIONFISH 7-14 in.

GREAT STAR CORAL   2-8 ft.

WHITESTAR SHEET CORAL   1-6 ft.

IVORY CORAL 4-30 in.

PILLAR CORAL 4-10 ft.

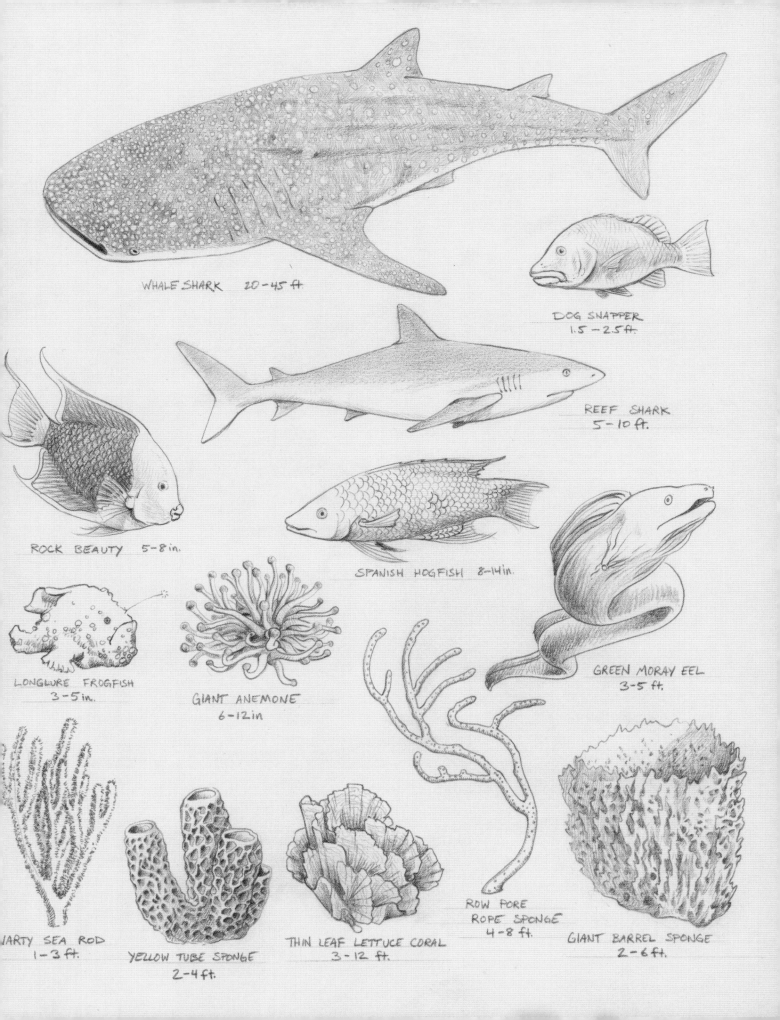

WHALE SHARK   20-45 ft.

DOG SNAPPER
1.5 - 2.5 ft.

REEF SHARK
5 - 10 ft.

ROCK BEAUTY   5-8 in.

SPANISH HOGFISH   8-14in.

GREEN MORAY EEL
3-5 ft.

LONGLURE FROGFISH
3-5 in.

GIANT ANEMONE
6-12in

WARTY SEA ROD
1-3 ft.

YELLOW TUBE SPONGE
2-4 ft.

THIN LEAF LETTUCE CORAL
3-12 ft.

ROW PORE
ROPE SPONGE
4-8 ft.

GIANT BARREL SPONGE
2-6 ft.

**JASON CHIN** is the author and artist of the award-winning book *Redwoods*, which *Kirkus Reviews* called "an inventive eye-opening adventure." His other work includes illustrations for Simon Winchester's *The Day the World Exploded*. He and his wife Deirdre, also an artist, live in Vermont with their children, Liam and Maeve.

# EXPLORE A COMPLEX ECOSYSTEM FULL OF THOUSANDS OF SPECIES

During an ordinary visit to the library, a girl pulls a not-so-ordinary book from the shelves. As she turns the pages in this book about coral reefs, the world around her slips away and she finds herself surrounded by the coral cities of the sea and the mysterious plants and animals that live, hunt, and hide there.

Meticulously researched and filled with gorgeous panoramas of the teeming worlds that lie beneath the seas, *Coral Reefs* is a worthy companion to Jason Chin's award-winning *Redwoods*.

---

⭐ "Chin, who pioneered this hybrid form of straightforward nonfiction text and fanciful pictures with *Redwoods* (2009), offers another statement about the power of reading for an imaginative child with this appealing introduction to a complex world." —*Kirkus Reviews*, starred review

"Information and fantasy collaborate in this imaginative introduction to coral reefs." —*The Bulletin*

"Chin offers a colorful and inventive introduction to coral reefs." —*School Library Journal*

"Offers a straightforward text discussing coral reefs, while the well-composed illustrations create an imaginative narrative running in parallel." —*Booklist*

*Also by Jason Chin*

AGES 5–9

SQUARE FISH
NEW YORK • MACKIDS.COM

US $8.99 / CAN $11.99
ISBN 978-1-250-07948-0

9 781250 079480

50899 >

The MAILBOX®

The Education Center®

TEC61111

R.F.

# Everything Numbers

grades PreK–K

- More than 160 tools to teach the numbers from 0 to 20
- Numeral–set–number word pages, a ready-to-use center, fold-and-go booklets, and more
- Prepares students for early math success

# About This Book

Using *Everything Numbers* in your classroom is as easy as 1, 2, 3! This all-in-one book features a collection of reproducible tools for teaching the numbers 0–20. It includes

- a numeral–set–number word page for each number 0–20
- a fold-and-go booklet for each number 0–10
- engaging practice pages that reinforce individual numbers
- counting games
- a number rhymes booklet
- a ready-to-use counting center
- 16 bonus activities

Every page is designed to prepare students for math success by **strengthening their understanding of number concepts, increasing number sense, and developing mathematical thinking.** When it comes to teaching numbers to your little learners, count on *Everything Numbers!*

If you have a book idea, we'd like to hear from you. See www.themailbox.com for submission guidelines.

## The MAILBOX® BOOKS

### We Started With Teachers and Their Students

- Teachers Jake and Marge Michel started The Education Center, Inc., publishing company in the basement of their North Carolina home. Their first product was a set of teacher idea cards stored in a cute canvas bag.
- In 1979, Jake and Marge started a new magazine comprised of ideas sent in by kindergarten–grade 6 teachers. It was called *The Mailbox*. Teachers loved it. Before long, *The Mailbox* was being used in classrooms by hundreds of thousands of teachers.
- Today *The Mailbox* is published in four editions, along with *Teacher's Helper*® magazine (also in four editions) and *The Mailbox*® BOOKBAG® magazine.

### We're Still All About Teachers and Their Students

- At The Mailbox Books, we understand that every minute counts in today's classroom. We've studied the state and national standards you are being held accountable for. From this research, we've identified the key skills students at your grade level are being required to learn. We build our books around these skills so that you can use them with the confidence that they'll help you reach your teaching goals.
- The Mailbox Books now offers over 450 titles for preschool–grade 6 teachers. These books can be found in over 1,000 teacher stores around the world.

The MAILBOX®